IMPRESSIONISM

IMPRESSIONISM

ODYSSEYS

JESSICA GUNDERSON

CREATIVE EDUCATION•CREATIVE PAPERBACKS

Published by Creative Education and Creative Paperbacks
P.O. Box 227, Mankato, Minnesota 56002
Creative Education and Creative Paperbacks
are imprints of The Creative Company
www.thecreativecompany.us

Design and production by Blue Design
Art direction by Rita Marshall
Printed in the United States of America

Photographs by The Bridgeman Art Library (Edgar Degas,
Edouard Manet, James Abbott McNeill Whistler), Getty
Images (Buyenlarge/Buyenlarge/Time Life Pictures, Paul
Cezanne, MIKE CLARKE/AFP, French School, Harlingue/Roger
Viollet, Ando or Utagawa Hiroshige, Hulton Archive, Hulton
Collection, Imagno, Edouard Manet, Clement Maurier, John
Miller, Claude Monet, Berthe Morisot, Camille Pissarro, Susanna
Price, Pierre Auguste Renoir, Roger Viollet Collection, Georges
Pierre Seurat, Stock Montage, Time Life Pictures/Mansell/Time
Life Pictures, James Abbott McNeill Whistler)

Library of Congress Cataloging-in-Publication Data
Gunderson, Jessica.
Impressionism / Jessica Gunderson.
p. cm. — (Odysseys in art)
Summary: An examination of the art movement known as
Impressionism from its beginnings in the 1860s to its decline
in the early 1900s, including an introduction to great artists
and works.
Includes bibliographical references and index.
ISBN 978-1-60818-533-7 (hardcover)
ISBN 978-1-62832-134-0 (pbk)
1. Impressionism (Art)—Juvenile literature. I. Title.

N6465.I4G86 2015
709.03'44—dc23   2014041721

CCSS: RI.8.1, 2, 3, 4; RI.9-10.1, 2, 3, 4; RI.11-12.1, 2, 3, 4

First Edition HC 9 8 7 6 5 4 3 2 1
First Edition PBK 9 8 7 6 5 4 3 2 1

Cover: *Claude Monet Reading* by Pierre Auguste Renoir (1872)
Page 2: *Harmony in Flesh Colour and Black: Portrait of Mrs.
Louise Jopling* by James McNeill Whistler (c. 1870s)
Pages 4–5: *Waterloo Bridge* by Claude Monet (1900)
Page 6: *Portrait de l'artiste (Self-Portrait)* by Paul Cézanne (c.
1875)

CONTENTS

Introduction

The history of the world can be told through accounts of great battles, the lives of kings and queens, and the discoveries and inventions of scientists and explorers. But the history of the way people think and feel about themselves and the world is told through art. From paintings of the hunt in prehistoric caves, to sacred art in the European Middle Ages, to the abstract forms of the 20th

OPPOSITE: Pierre Auguste Renoir was much sought after as a painter of portraits. In *Portrait of the Actress Jeanne Samary* (1877), Renoir characteristically bathes the canvas with light and color and captures his friend in a candid expression.

century, movements in art are the expression of a culture. Sometimes that expression is so powerful and compelling that it reaches through time to carry its message to another generation.

In the 1860s, a group of painters and writers met frequently at a small Paris café to discuss the state of art. They spoke passionately against the principles of art tradition. Art, they believed, should be about **sensory** perceptions and should not rely wholly on subject matter as it had in the past. What was a subject without the paint with which it was depicted? What was life but a series of fleeting moments? Their questions led to debates that lasted long into the night. At the time, the artists didn't know that their **philosophies** would transform into a strong and lasting movement—Impressionism—that would change the art world forever.

From Realism to Impressionism

The 19th century was an era of great social and cultural transformation in Europe and other parts of the globe. The **Industrial Revolution** that had begun in the 1700s had caused rural dwellers to migrate to the city for factory employment and had given rise to new, quicker methods of transportation, such as the passenger train. By the second half of the 1800s, some monarchies had been replaced by democratic governments, and because of such shifts in political power and government, the lines between social classes blurred. The aristocracy and upper class no longer held as much power over society, and as a result, the middle class grew in social and economic strength.

The lower working class, however, still struggled with poverty. A growing awareness of the plight of the impoverished working class led to revolutions and protests that urged social change.

France, especially, was a cauldron of rebellion and political upheaval. In the early 1800s, Napoleon I exerted his rule over the French and sought to expand his empire into other parts of Europe. After Napoleon fell from power in 1815, monarchy was reinstated in France, but the Revolution of 1848 led to a democratic government, which was taken over by Napoleon III in 1852.

Against this turbulent backdrop, art in Paris, the cultural center of Europe, thrived. The government-funded Royal Academy of Painting and Sculpture controlled the art world with its competitive exhibitions, called Salons, as well as its inclination toward traditional styles, such as symmetrical compositions and smooth surfaces, and traditional subject matter, such as religion or Classical Roman and Greek gods. The artists of the Realist movement in midcentury broke away from these traditions by painting contemporary, everyday events.

The Impressionist movement, a French painting movement that was centered in Paris, sprang from Realism, thanks largely to a prominent painter of the time, Edouard Manet (1832–83). Manet was a Realist in the sense that he wanted to capture the current moment, but he was also ready to break away from conventional methods of painting. As a student, he had quarreled with his teacher because he felt that modeling and painting could be done out-of-doors. His teacher was shocked at the idea because it defied the tradition of painting inside a studio.

His unconventional ideas led Manet to paint the highly controversial *Luncheon on the Grass* (1863), which became the seed of the Impressionist movement. The painting was rejected from the Salon of 1863, but so many paintings by other artists had also been rejected that Napoleon III organized the *Salon des Refusés* (Salon of the Rejected). Even here, though, *Luncheon on the Grass* stirred up debate. The scene of two fully-clothed men and two women, one scantily clothed and one nude, casually picnicking in the woods was controversial in itself, but

The Eiffel Tower

In preparation for the 1889 World's Fair (an event featuring exhibits of manufactured products and inventions from various countries), the Parisian government **commissioned** sculptor Gustave Eiffel to build a tower at the entrance of the fairgrounds. The Eiffel Tower took two years to construct and was the tallest structure in the world for more than 40 years. Standing 1,052 feet (320.8 m) tall, the tower is today one of the most famous landmarks in Europe. But the tower was not built without controversy. As it was being erected, more than 300 Parisians, including writer and friend of the Impressionists Émile Zola, signed a petition against its construction, decrying it as tasteless, monstrous, and a disgrace to the city.

one of the major debates over the painting had to do with Manet's style. He used broad brushstrokes that relied on the juxtaposition of different colors to create depth. He did not try to hide the brushstrokes to make the image appear real; instead, he believed that the viewer should see the paint on the canvas. He focused on light and wanted his brushstrokes to replicate the way light fell on the scene. Manet believed that the hand should be an extension of the eye. He was more concerned with what was being seen than with the thoughts or ideas behind the painting. Though Manet never exhibited with the Impressionists nor considered himself a part of their movement, he is regarded as a father of Impressionist painting because of his innovative ideas.

Manet was part of a group of artists and writers who met at the Café Guerbois in Paris to discuss the state of art. Many of these artists had been rejected from the Academy Salons, and they in turn rejected the traditional ideas of the Academy. In 1869, two painters of the group, Claude Monet (1840–1926) and Pierre Auguste Renoir (1841–1919) developed a method of applying paint in short strokes of color. This method soon became representative of the new Impressionist technique. Monet and Renoir studied the reflection of the sky on water and how shadows changed nearby colors. They wanted their brushstrokes to imitate the liveliness and changing mood of light, and their short, quick spots of paint achieved their goal. This method of applying paint was radical and

nontraditional, and therefore the other members of the group embraced it.

n 1870, the Parisian group's meetings were interrupted by the Franco-Prussian War. As the fighting drew closer to Paris, many of the artists left the country. Monet, along with artist Camille Pissarro (1830–1903), fled to London, where the two became close friends, often painting together out-of-doors. In 1871, France and Prussia signed a peace treaty, and the Impressionist artists returned to Paris and resumed their work.

Upon their return to France, Monet and Pissarro urged their fellow painters to hold an exhibition separate from the Salon, and in 1874, the group held its first show at artist Nadar's (1820–1910) photography studio. Crowds flocked to the exhibition, but most of the viewers and critics mocked the paintings, calling them sketch-like and unfinished. Many people felt that art should help unite the country after the devastation of war and said that the artists' nontraditional paintings were not what the country needed. Critic Louis Leroy was the first to call these painters Impressionists, taking the word from the title of Monet's painting *Impression, Sunrise* (1872). He had meant the term to be insulting, indicating that the paintings were mere impressions of the world rather than deeply deliberated renderings, but the group took on the name in a positive way, using it to promote their work and exhibitions. Eight Impressionist exhibitions were held in Paris between 1874 and 1886, and by 1886, the Impressionists were considered serious artists.

Avoiding subjects such as politics or religion, most Impressionists focused on the leisure of the middle class, painting the activities of cafés, parks, theaters, and ballets. Country life as well as city life was depicted in their paintings. Advancements in transportation, such as the railroad, allowed Impressionists to travel easily to the countryside, and the recent invention of transportable tubes of pre-mixed paint freed them from having to work near their studios.

Impressionist painters concerned themselves with the study of color and light. They believed that color is changed by its surroundings, such as light, other objects, and nearby colors. Instead of blending paints, they juxtaposed colors to achieve the desired hue. For example, a yellow stroke of paint next to a blue stroke of paint achieved the effect of green.

Impressionists were more interested in light's effects on the eye than in subject matter or the true, physical description of objects. Manet believed that the viewer should look at the painting or canvas itself rather than at what it depicted, and the Impressionists adopted his viewpoint. Their task was to show the fleeting moment, and in order to paint quickly enough to capture that moment, they developed speed and mobility in their technique. They rejected all subjects that could not be perceived by their senses. For the Impressionists, painting became a sensory experience.

1870s Paris

Impressionist artists in Paris often portrayed the life and leisure of the upper-middle class, which experienced growing authority in the 19th century as the aristocracy lost much of its governing power. During the 1870s, Paris was the fashion capital of the world, and members of the upper-middle class attended theaters, operas, ballets, and circuses dressed in the most fashionable styles of the times. Women wore dresses with bustled skirts and ruffled sleeves, and men wore top hats, vests, and frock coats, or long jackets. Today, Paris remains a center for art and fashion.

25

Artists of the Impressionist Movement

The artist who most exemplified the Impressionist movement's ideals was Claude Monet, the leader of the group. Born in Paris in 1840, Monet spent his childhood in the seaside port of Le Havre, where he studied with French landscape artist Eugene Boudin (1824–98). As an adult, Monet moved to Paris, but he continued

OPPOSITE: Claude Monet, pictured around 1900, valued art forms from other cultures and collected ancient figurines as well as Japanese woodblock prints—he had amassed 231 such prints by the end of his life.

to paint landscapes, his primary focus being color. Color, he once said, was his "daylong obsession, joy, and torment." Monet experimented with juxtaposing colors to create the effect of light and shadow. From his observations of the world, he concluded that shadows could look dark blue or red or green or any number of colors, depending on the colors around them and the light that reflected from the objects. He painted more than 40 views of one cathedral, each at a different time of day, so that he could capture the correspondingly different light effects. Around the year 1870, he eliminated dark colors from his palette and worked exclusively with light ones.

Monet did not focus on conceptual ideas and subject matter; instead, he focused solely on the sensory images in front of him—what his eyes saw. For example, the painting *Poppies, near Argenteuil* (1873) depicts

Monet's wife and son walking in a field; however, rather than represent them as fully formed figures that have meaning to the artist, the two appear as merely dabs of paint among the brilliant poppies.

Monet's close friend Camille Pissarro was a somewhat older member of the Impressionists and was the only artist to display his work in all eight Impressionist exhibitions. Like Monet, Pissarro believed that light and color were essential to nature, and he often painted *en plein air*, or outdoors. Also like Monet, he experimented with painting the same scene in different conditions: light and dark, rain and sunshine. He had a rolling studio—an easel with wheels and drawers for supplies—built so that he could move around outdoors with ease. Although Pissarro's artistic philosophy was similar to Monet's, his style differed from that of his friend. While Monet emphasized quick brushstrokes and blurred images, Pissarro emphasized the use of clear, firm lines in many of his paintings. As he grew older, he developed an eye condition that made him so sensitive to sunlight that he could no longer paint outdoors, and he turned to depicting views of Paris from various windows around the city.

Pierre Auguste Renoir was another close friend of Monet's. The two shared a studio in Paris when they were young artists still finding their styles. Renoir began his career painting designs on porcelain cups and plates, but that job was soon taken over by machines, so he began painting portraits to make money. He loved portraying the human figure and was influenced by Monet to emphasize the effects of light on images in his work. He combined his interest in natural light effects with his love of the figure, as is evident in his painting

The Franco-Prussian War

France declared war on Prussia, a German state, in 1870, after Spain offered its throne to a member of the Prussian royalty. Napoleon III, the leader of France, believed that Prussia was building an empire, and he wished to stop Prussia's growth. The chancellor of Prussia, Otto von Bismarck (above), implored nearby German states to aid in the war. In August 1870, German troops began their march into France, defeating French troops along the way. In September, the Germans surrounded Paris, and a siege of the city began. Many Parisians, including some artists, had fled the city before the Germans arrived. Those who stayed endured months of hunger until an armistice was signed in February 1871.

Luncheon of the Boating Party (1881). The scene shows people laughing, talking, and flirting as sunlight weaves through the trees to shine upon them. The sun fits in perfectly with the joyful mood of the painting. Renoir liked to capture happy moments in his paintings. "Life was a perpetual holiday," he later said. "The world knew how to laugh in those days."

Berthe Morisot (1841–95) was one of only a few prominent female French Impressionist painters. During the 18th and 19th centuries, watercolor and drawing were considered pleasurable pastimes for women, who usually painted only in an amateur role, but Morisot was a serious artist who did not give up painting for domestic life. She was a student of landscape artist Camille Corot (1796–1875) and met Edouard Manet while she was studying paintings at the Louvre Museum in Paris. She often modeled for him and later married his brother. Morisot developed an individualized style despite the influence of Manet and other Impressionist artists. Her brushstrokes were light and delicate and her colors gentle. Because it was not acceptable for women to be alone in the company of men, Morisot often painted scenes of children and women. One of her goals was to show that women had a unique and valid outlook on the world that could be translated to art. She remained faithful to the Impressionist style throughout her life and never strayed from her vision.

Degas was interested in portraying people and the movement of the human body.

French artist Edgar Degas (1834–1917) never considered himself an Impressionist, but he often exhibited his work with the group and met with them at the Café Guerbois. He was an aristocrat by birth and was trained in the Classical, academic tradition, which influenced his approach to painting throughout his career. Degas was interested in portraying people and the movement of the human body. His paintings often depicted the ballet, theater, horseracing, and opera. He never painted landscapes, nor did he paint outdoors. Instead, he chose to focus on the effects of artificial, indoor lighting from gas lamps and candles. He often used photographs as studies for his work, and his paintings have a photographic feel, with some objects cut off at the edge rather than perfectly framed. Degas' subjects of ballet rehearsals and horseracing had never before been depicted in art, and his approach to his subjects was revolutionary. He loved to capture the strenuous work that goes into the production of a ballet or an opera, and his paintings often portray figures in the midst of movement. When his eyesight began to fail, Degas turned to sculpture and experimented with sculpting bodies in various forms of motion.

American painter Mary Cassatt (1844–1926) was a friend of Degas', and his work influenced her throughout her career. She studied at the Pennsylvania Academy of Fine Arts in Philadelphia, and in 1866, she left America to settle in Paris, where she met Degas, whose inspiration can be seen in her use of prominent lines. Like fellow female artist Morisot, Cassatt drew from domestic subjects such as children and women. Members of her own family were often models for her work. She contributed greatly to the acceptance of Impressionist art in the United States by setting up exhibitions there and encouraging her American friends to buy Impressionist paintings. Of Cassatt's work, Degas said, "I will not admit that a woman can draw so well."

British Impressionist Alfred Sisley (1839–99) is often overlooked becasue of the similarity of his work to Monet's. Born in France to English parents, Sisley lived and worked in France for most of his life. Because his work was compared with Monet's, and Monet's was often considered superior, Sisley never made much money on his art during his lifetime. While Monet often chose dramatic or vibrantly colored subjects such as the ocean and flower gardens, Sisley focused on softer-toned landscapes, as is evident in one of his most famous works, *The Bridge at Moret-sur-Loing* (1893). Unlike many other Impressionists who later strayed from the core principles of Impressionism, Sisley remained true to the Impressionist technique of using quick brush-strokes and portraying the atmospheric effects of light throughout his career.

The Motion Picture

In 1895, French brothers and inventors Louis and Auguste Lumiere (above) developed the first motion picture camera. They based their invention on the kinetoscope, a type of camera that rapidly advanced a strip of film frame by frame to produce the illusion of motion. The Lumiere brothers combined the kinetoscope with a light projector to display the moving pictures, or movies, on a screen. Pianists played along with the motion pictures, and later, recorded music was played with the film. In 1919, Lee de Forest created Phonofilm, the method of putting sound on film, and by 1930, almost all motion pictures had sound.

Great Works of Impressionism

Claude Monet's *Impression, Sunrise*, the piece that gave the Impressionists their name, caused quite an uproar at the First Impressionist Exhibition of 1874. The painting shows the harbor of Le Havre, Monet's boyhood home. But rather than depicting its realistic details in Classical landscape tradition, Monet used sparse, minimal brushstrokes to

FOLLOWING PAGES: "Landscape is nothing but an impression, and an instantaneous one," said Monet in describing his painting *Impression, Sunrise*. Although disparaged by its contemporary critics, it became one of the most highly valued pieces of Impressionist art.

Monet used sparse, minimal brushstrokes to set down the bare essentials of the scene ...

set down the bare essentials of the scene, capturing the atmosphere, mood, light, and time of day of the harbor. The scene is one that will disappear in a moment, and Monet was able to transfer that fleeting moment onto his canvas. As in many of his paintings, Monet shows the sunlight's effects on water. The rising sun glows red over the harbor, reflected in fragments on the water's surface, and a morning mist shrouds the masts of drifting boats. Although the painting gained harsh criticism from art reviewers for its evidently quick strokes of paint and its sketch-like feel, today it is revered as one of the first pieces to encapsulate the characteristics of the Impressionist movement.

IMPRESSIONISM

As much as Monet loved to depict light on water, Pierre Auguste Renoir loved to portray the human figure, as in his 1876 painting *Ball at the Moulin de la Galette*. The painting's setting is the courtyard at the Moulin de la Galette, an old mill that had been turned into a dance hall. In Renoir's painting, members of the middle class are gathered in the courtyard, dancing, talking, laughing, and flirting. The viewer is drawn in by a group of friends in the lower right-hand corner, in the foreground of the canvas, but there is no true focal point of the piece, so the viewer's gaze flits from group to group. Couples are shown in various stages of dance, and the sense of movement, music, and light is convincing to the eye. Like other Impressionists, Renoir was interested in the effects of light, and in this piece, light falls through the trees onto the friends and dancers. The painting is unified by sunlight, mood, and the abundance of purples and blues. Renoir did not use sharp lines and edges to shape the objects and figures in the painting; rather, he used light, shade, and color to set the contours.

L ike Renoir, Edgar Degas had a passion for portraying figures, but Degas placed much emphasis on the use of line. In his painting *The Rehearsal* (c. 1877), he used diagonal lines across the dance floor to give a sense of movement to the rehearsing ballerinas. His use of line was inspired by 18th-century Japanese woodblock prints, which had

Edgar Degas took inspiration from Japanese artwork's sense of movement, which he transferred to his paintings of French ballet dancers.

recently been discovered and recognized by European artists. Degas' piece has a photographic feel to it; objects, such as the spiral staircase, are not perfectly displayed but are cut off by the edges of the frame. The windows in the background and the dancers in the foreground exude the sense of a large space. There is no central focus, which allows the viewer to look into the scene from various angles.

Although Mary Cassatt was largely influenced by Degas, she also had her own style. She often used motherhood as her theme, as in *The Bath* (1891–92), which shows a mother giving her child a bath. In many of her pieces, Cassatt gives motherhood a sense of dignity, as she does in this painting. She emphasizes line in *The Bath* with the woman's striped dress and the outline of the washbasin. Similar colors bring the mother, child,

There is no central focus, which allows the viewer to look into the scene from various angles.

and washbasin together against the darkness of the floor. Red undertones give the child's and the mother's skin a warm, lively essence. Like Degas, Cassatt was influenced by the study of Japanese woodblock prints.

Camille Pissarro's *Hillside of the Hermitage, Pontoise* (1873) represents his unique approach to landscape. Pissarro painted *Hillside of the Hermitage* near his home in Pontoise, a small town about 25 miles (40 km) from Paris. In this piece, Pissarro did not use the scope of a traditional landscape—a wide view of the land and sky; instead, he zoomed in on the hillside and represented it from close proximity. The sky is almost nonexistent due to the rising crest of the hill. The houses and surrounding terrain are portrayed with block-like shapes and small, wide strokes of paint.

onet's painting, *On the Bank of the Seine, Bennecourt* (1868), also shows landscape in a non-traditional way. In the painting, a woman sits along the banks of the Seine River, the canopy of a tree shading her. The tree also obscures the view of the village across the river. Only small bits of houses and other buildings can be seen. However, the village is reflected on the surface of the river, and the buildings are detailed and bright.

Montmartre

The neighborhood of Montmartre in northern Paris served as the center of entertainment life in the mid-1800s, and by the end of the century, it had become one of the principal artistic centers of Paris. Artists such as Camille Pissarro, Claude Monet, and Henri de Toulouse-Lautrec inhabited Montmartre and depicted the area in their paintings. Today, the Moulin de la Galette, the subject of paintings by Pierre Auguste Renoir and Toulouse-Lautrec, still stands as a historical landmark. Other landmarks include the Basilica of the Sacre Couer, a famous church on Montmartre Hill, and the Moulin Rouge, a famous **cabaret** hall. Many famous artists, including Edgar Degas, are buried in Montmartre's cemetery.

The painting caused one critic to state that it was as if Whistler had flung paint on the canvas and called it art.

The reflection appears just as real as the actual village, exemplifying Monet's fascination with light upon water.

American artist James McNeill Whistler (1834–1903), who lived much of his life in Europe, combined Impressionist theories with his own. He often focused on contemporary life and the sensation of color. Whistler's painting *Nocturne in Black and Gold: The Falling Rocket* (1875) shows the influence of Impressionism, as swirls and dots of gold dance across a dark background of layered tones, representing the movement of fireworks and stars against a stormy night sky. The painting caused one critic to state that it was as if Whistler had flung paint on the canvas and called it art. Whistler sued the critic for libel and won the case, although he accumulated a huge debt from court fees in the process.

Edouard Manet's final masterpiece, *A Bar at the Folies-Bergère* (1882), was painted during the time he associated with the Impressionists. All his life, Manet had longed for academic acceptance, and he painted the nearly life-sized *A Bar at the Folies-Bergère* as a modern representation of a Classical Salon masterpiece. The scene is of an ordinary barmaid behind a bar; her

A Bar at the Folies-Bergère was the last major work Manet completed before his death in 1883. Drawing inspiration from 17th-century Spanish painter Diego Velázquez, Manet produced a modern translation of Velázquez's reflective masterpiece *Las Meninas* (1656).

Japonisme

In the last half of the 19th century, an interest in Japanese prints and decorative arts swept through Europe. In 1854, Japanese ports had opened to Western trade, and Japanese prints, trinkets, fans, and lacquers—art pieces in which bits of metal, usually gold or silver, are sprinkled onto wet lacquer—flooded the European market. The fascination with Japanese art grew so intense that in 1872 the French term *Japonisme*—referring to Japanese art and culture and its influence—was coined. Many artists, such as Claude Monet, Edouard Manet, and Edgar Degas, began collecting Japanese pieces and displaying them in their homes and studios, where the pieces often influenced their own art, especially in respect to line and color.

weariness is evident on her face. Behind her, a mirror reflects the crowded room of the establishment. In the upper left-hand corner, the feet of a trapeze artist dangle. However, none of the customers seems to be watching the spectacle. The barmaid herself is reflected in the mirror as she serves a customer. There is a great contrast between her actual image and her reflection; in the reflection she does not look bored. Instead, she leans toward the customer in a familiar way. Critics and historians have debated Manet's intentions. Some say he wished to contrast human longing and the dream of happiness with the reality of ordinary life. Others say that his inclusion of a mirror was a comment that a painting is, and should be, a reflection of society.

Manet's painting was a response to the ideas of the Impressionist movement. He focused on various light effects. Reflected light spills from glass globes onto the customers and bottles. *A Bar at the Folies-Bergère* is more serious than other Impressionist pieces, in part because Manet used a wide spectrum of colors, including black, a color most Impressionist painters avoided. Like other Impressionists, though, Manet captured the instant of a passing moment with the solidity of a masterpiece.

The Resonance of Impressionism

By the 1880s, the Impressionist style had become accepted within the academic Salons and was gaining popularity among the public as well. Well-known galleries displayed and sold Impressionist paintings. But even as their style gained recognition, and perhaps because of it, some Impressionists grew discontent. They felt that they were no longer at the forefront of innovation and that too many traditional aspects of art were being overlooked in the search for sensory perceptions and truths. Camille Pissarro, in particular, was dissatisfied with the lack of disciplined method in Impressionism. Some historians refer to this period of change as the "Crisis of Impressionism."

Pierre Auguste Renoir was one artist to shift away from the philosophies of Impressionism. He felt that painting the fleeting moment would cause the painting itself to have fleeting importance. Confining art to his own time, he believed, would not allow it to resonate through future generations. By the mid-1880s, Renoir felt that he had "wrung Impressionism dry." He began painting his figures in a more timeless, Classical style. Rather than using fuzzy shapes and loose brushstrokes, Renoir gave his figures a clarity and solidity that he felt would give them permanence in the art world.

Even Claude Monet, the leader of Impressionism, seemed to be searching for a way to give the style more permanence. In the 1890s, he made numerous studies of the same scenes, among them the Rouen Cathedral in northwestern France, at various times of day. While this act represented his love of light effects, it also reflected the fact that he found a certain permanence in the objects he painted. No matter the time of day, the Rouen Cathedral would be the same object, illustrating a stability in even the brief, passing moment. Monet's choice of subject matter, too, took on more historical significance, similar to that of academic painters. The Rouen Cathedral was a religious icon similar to other religious icons that had been depicted in art through the ages, and poplar trees, known as "Liberty Trees," which he painted many times, were also significant in French history. People started planting them during the French Revolution in 1790 to represent French democracy.

In each of the Impressionist exhibitions during the 1880s, new, young artists brought forth their work. The inclusion of up-and-coming artists in the exhibitions, as well as the growing acceptance of the Impressionist style, signified that Impressionism was gaining status and breaking new ground. Some of Impressionism's new artists influenced the older generation; Pissarro, for example,

By the mid-1880s, Renoir felt that he had "wrung Impressionism dry." He began painting his figures in a more timeless, Classical style.

experimented with smaller, tighter brushstrokes in his later paintings, a technique he learned from some of the younger artists. Paul Cézanne (1839–1906), a French painter who was part of the Impressionist movement, was never completely satisfied with the Impressionist viewpoint and melded the ideas of Impressionism with his own theories of color and the physicality of objects. Cézanne and four other painters—French artists Georges Seurat (1859–91), Henri de Toulouse-Lautrec (1864–1901), and Paul Gauguin (1848–1903), and Dutch artist Vincent van Gogh (1853–90)—became leaders of the movement that sprang from Impressionism: Post-Impressionism.

The Post-Impressionists were not the close-knit group that the Impressionists were, and the artists' styles were quite different, but each had a basis in Impressionism. Post-Impressionism was both an extension of Impressionism and a rejection of some of its ideas. Post-Impressionists used bright, vibrant colors and detailed daily life, as the Impressionists had, but they often emphasized expressiveness and geometric form over the effects of light. Cézanne, for example, shared the Impressionists' love of color, but he was fascinated not only with the color of objects but also with the objects themselves. He experimented with new ways to portray objects, which led to his move toward abstract art—art with images that do not represent the physical truth of objects. Van Gogh, too, was influenced by the Impressionist color palette, but rather than using color to express sensation, van Gogh used it to express his inner feelings and desires. He attached meaning to certain colors; for example, to him, the color yellow signified happiness. But color was not the only influencing factor of Impressionism: Toulouse-Lautrec's use of line was directly inspired by Edgar Degas, though the lines in Toulouse-Lautrec's work serve to both outline a shape and take on a shape of their own. With each of the Post-Impressionist artists, the ideas of the Impressionists took root, grew, and changed into unique, significant styles.

Georges Seurat took painting to a more scientific level with his studies in pointillism, which is also called divisionism, and created a masterpiece of the form in *Sunday Afternoon on the Île de la Grande Jatte* (1884–86).

A t the height of Impressionism and Post-Impressionism, scientific thought paralleled art's concentration on sensory perception as a way of interpreting the physical world. Physicists, philosophers, and psychologists believed that sensation is reality and that knowledge must be based on the analysis of human sensory perceptions. But as new scientific thought emerged in the early 20th

TAKEAWAY

Van Gogh, in particular, focused on the internal reality of his emotions and aimed to transfer that reality to the canvas.

century, artists changed the way they depicted the world. In 1905, Albert Einstein began publicizing his theory of relativity, which states that the reality of any object must be considered relative to the positions of both the object being observed and the observer. Because the world is made up of space and time, which cannot be measured with true exactness, Einstein's theory held that objects are perceived differently by different observers. This theory led to new artistic ideas about perception, as painters considered the effect of their emotions and ideas on the images they portrayed. Van Gogh, in particular, focused on the internal reality of his emotions and aimed to transfer that reality to the canvas. He used the quick, loose brushstrokes of the Impressionists to reveal his inner state of mind, and his ideas led to the later movement of Expressionism, which focused on the expression of emotions through art.

OPPOSITE Faced with disappointing circumstances many times over, Vincent van Gogh did not pursue a career in art until the final decade of his life. During those 10 years, though, he produced more than 2,000 works, including many self-portraits, and developed a distinctive style that would influence the course of art in the 20th century.

The 20th century also brought about new inventions that transformed the world that the Impressionists had portrayed in their paintings. Telephones, automobiles, the motion picture camera, and the radio were invented around the turn of the century, changing the way people communicated and traveled. The leisurely activities of the late 1800s, such as boating and picnicking, were no longer as popular as moviegoing and radio-listening. Visual art reflected the changing world, as young artists, like the Impressionists before them, stripped art of its conventional subjects. Form, color, and shape alone became justifications for art; no longer were traditional, tangible subjects important to a painting or sculpture. Thanks to the success of Impressionism as a movement and a technique, artists felt liberated from the constraints of the Academy and the Salon exhibitions. Abstract art,

Marmottan Museum

The Marmottan Museum in Paris boasts the largest collection of Claude Monet's paintings in the world, and an entire section of the museum is dedicated to the founding painters of the Impressionist movement. More than 300 Impressionist and Post-Impressionist paintings, pastels, watercolors, and sculptures are on display at the Marmottan Museum, including Berthe Morisot's *At the Ball* (1875), Camille Pissarro's *The Outer Boulevards* (1879), and Monet's *Impression, Sunrise*. In addition to Impressionist works, visitors can view art of early 19th-century France as well as works from the **medieval** period, such as illuminated manuscripts, stained glass, and furniture.

fathered by Paul Cézanne, emerged in the early 20th century as a forceful style of painting and sculpture. The modern age had dawned, and with it came changes in attitudes about art.

At Impressionism's height, many artists and critics questioned whether the movement could have lasting value, but time has shown that indeed it has. Paintings from the movement are among the most popular art pieces today, and almost all contemporary styles of painting can trace their roots back to Impressionism. With their emphasis on what is seen in the painting rather than what is represented, Impressionists paved the way for innovations in technique and subject that allowed modern art to evolve.

Monet's House and Gardens at Giverny

One of Claude Monet's favorite subjects in his later years was the water garden at his home in Giverny, a village outside of Paris, where he lived for 43 years. Today, visitors to the home can view the water garden—as well as several other gardens—that inspired Monet's later pieces, such as *Water Lilies and Japanese Bridge* (1899), *Water Lilies* (1906), *Wisteria* (1920), and *The House from the Garden* (1922). Many of the flowering plants, such as the wisteria, that decorate the grounds today were planted by Monet.

Timeline

1840   Tubes of oil paint are invented

1854   Japanese ports open to Western trade

1859   Claude Monet arrives in Paris

1860   Monet and Camille Pissarro meet

1863   Edouard Manet shows *Luncheon on the Grass* at the *Salon des Refusés*

1869   Monet and Pierre Auguste Renoir develop the Impressionist painting technique

1870   The Franco-Prussian War begins, and Monet and Pissarro leave France, returning when the war ends the next year

1872   Monet completes *Impression, Sunrise*, the piece that gives Impressionism its name

1874   The First Impressionist Exhibition is held

1876   Alexander Graham Bell invents and patents the telephone in the U.S.; Renoir paints *Ball at the Moulin de la Galette*

1879   The electric light bulb is invented

1883   Manet dies at the age of 51; Monet relocates to Giverny

1884   Berthe Morisot paints *Little Girl with a Doll*

1886   The Eighth (and final) Impressionist Exhibition is held

1889   The Eiffel Tower is built for the World's Fair in Paris

1891–92   Mary Cassatt paints *The Bath*

1894 Monet paints the *Rouen Cathedral* series

1895 The motion picture camera is invented

1900 Renoir receives the Legion of Honor award, the highest artistic award in France

1922 Monet paints *The House from the Garden*

Bibliography

Cole, Bruce, and Adelheid Gealt. *Art of the Western World: From Ancient Greece to Post-Modernism*. New York: Simon & Schuster, 1989.

Gardner, Louise. *Art through the Ages*. Orlando, Fla.: Harcourt Brace, 1991.

Gilbert, Rita, and William McCarter. *Living with Art*. 2nd ed. New York: Knopf, 1985.

Hanson, Lawrence, and Elisabeth Hanson. *Impressionism: Golden Decade*. New York: Holt, Rinehart and Winston, 1961.

Jaffe, Hans L. C. *The World of the Impressionists*. Maplewood, N.J.: Hammond, 1969.

Pool, Phoebe. *Impressionism*. London: Thames and Hudson, 1967.

Thomson, Belinda, and Michael Howard. *Impressionism*. New York: Exeter Books, 1988.

Wildenstein, Daniel. *Monet's Years at Giverny: Beyond Impressionism*. New York: Metropolitan Museum of Art, 1978.

Glossary

academic
conforming to the rules of an academy, or society of scholars or artists, such as the Royal Academy of Painting and Sculpture in France

amateur
someone who does something for pleasure rather than for a career

aristocracy
the group of people of the highest social rank, often the wealthy or descendants of royalty

cabaret
an establishment that provides food, drinks, a dance hall, and entertainment shows

commissioned
paid to do work for someone

democratic
having to do with a system of government in which leaders are elected by the people

economic
having to do with the way money, goods, and services affect a society

icon
an image or symbol

Industrial Revolution
a period of time from the mid-1700s to the early 1900s in which machines replaced work done by hand and new methods of transportation were developed

juxtaposition
the placement of two things side by side, especially to compare or contrast them

leisure	free time, when one does not have to work or study
medieval	having to do with the Middle Ages, a period in Europe between from the 5th to the 15th century A.D.
monarchies	types of governments that are ruled by royalty, often a king or queen
palette	the colors or kinds of colors used by an artist
philosophies	ideas and beliefs about certain subjects, such as truth, wisdom, the nature of reality, and knowledge
sensory	having to do with the five senses: taste, touch, smell, hearing, and sight
symmetrical	having matching points, parts, or shapes on both sides of a dividing line
theme	the main subject or idea of a piece of art

Index